TELLING THE TIME

My Day at the Park

ticktock

By Alice Proctor

Copyright © ticktock Entertainment Ltd 2007
First published in Great Britain in 2007 by ticktock Media Ltd.,
Unit 2, Orchard Business Centre, North Farm Road,
Tunbridge Wells, Kent, TN2 3XF

ticktock project editor: Julia Adams
ticktock project designer: Emma Randall
ticktock picture researcher: Lizzie Knowles

We would like to thank: Jo Hanks, Debra Voege, Colin Beer, Rebecca Clunes

ISBN 978 1 84696 482 4 pbk

Printed in China

Picture credits
t = top, b = bottom, c = centre, l = left, r = right, OFC = outside front cover, OBC = outside back cover

Alamy: 11. Banana Stock: 6t, 13b, 16, 17t, 19b, OBCtr, OBCcr, OBCbr. Gettyimages/Michael Wildsmith: 8.
Jupiter Images (Banana Stock): 18, 19t. Photolibrary/ Creatas: 10t. Shutterstock: 1, 4, 5, 9t, 13t, 14, 23,
OFCr. Superstock: 9r, 10r, 12, 15b, 17b. Ticktock Media Archive: 6b, 7, 8bc, 15t, 20, 21, 22, OFCl, OBCl,
OBC far right x3.

Every effort has been made to trace the copyright holders, and we apologise in advance for any unintentional
omissions. We would be pleased to insert the appropriate acknowledgements in any subsequent edition
of this publication.

Contents

Words in **bold** are explained in the glossary!

What makes a day?

A day is 24 hours long. It has a daytime and a night time. These are the all the parts of a day.

Morning and afternoon

Morning is the first part of the **day**. It is when the Sun rises. It ends at **noon**, or 12 **o'clock**. This is when the Sun is high in the sky.

The next part of the day is called **afternoon**. This part lasts from noon until dinner time.

Evening and night time

Evening starts when you finish dinner, at about 6 o'clock. This is when the Sun is getting low in the sky. This means it is getting dark outside.

When the Sun has set, then it is **night** time. Now it is dark outside and you can see the Moon and stars.

Which part of the day is it now?

Telling the time

It is my birthday on Sunday. My friends are going to meet me in the park at 12 o'clock.

Let's check we can tell the time, so we know when they are coming.

Two hands

This clock has two hands. The little hand is called the **hour** hand. Look, it is pointing at the 9.

The big hand is called the **minute** hand. It is pointing at the 12, so the time is exactly 9 o'clock.

2 o'clock

On this clock, the little hand is pointing at the 2. The big hand is pointing at the 12. Now the time is exactly 2 o'clock.

Digital clocks

Digital clocks have no hands. They have two numbers. The first number tells us the hour. On this clock, the hour is 8. The second number tells us the minutes past the hour. On this clock it is 0 minutes past the hour. This means it is exactly 8 o'clock.

Each hour starts when the big hand is at the 12.

My day at the park

My alarm clock rings. It is finally Sunday, and today is my birthday! I am really looking forward to going to the park for my party.

Time to wake-up!

7 o'clock

It is sunny outside. Time to get up and get dressed. I put on my favourite clothes.

I hope all my friends remember it is my party today. We are going to have a great time!

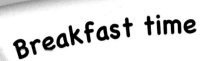

Breakfast time

I eat my breakfast.
Cereal and orange juice
is my favourite breakfast.

Cards and presents

8 o'clock

Look, here's the postman. What
has he got for me? I get eight
birthday cards, a Frisbee,
toy cars and some books.

When is your birthday?

My birthday morning

Here are Grandma and Grandpa. They are coming to my party, too.

A very special present

9 o'clock

Grandma and Grandpa say their special present is waiting for me outside. I wonder what it can be?

Wow! Look at my new bike. Let's cycle to the park.

Ready to go?

10 o'clock

Mum, Grandma and Grandpa say they have lots to carry. They are going to drive to the park. Dad says he will cycle there with me.

Let's see how long it takes us to get to the park. Come on, Dad, keep up!

Don't forget your cycle helmet when you ride your bike!

Picnic in the the park

It is quite warm now. It is a perfect day for a party in the park.

Ready for a party?

11 o'clock

Mum and Grandma find a lovely spot in the picnic area. They set the table for my party. Wow! Look at all of that food.

We are going to have a treasure hunt. I wonder what the prize will be?

Here are my friends!

12 o'clock

It is noon. Justin and Michael are the first people to arrive at my party. When everybody else has arrived, we start our treasure hunt.

Pirates' treasure

After an hour, my friend Michael finds the treasure. It is some chocolate coins! Michael shares the chocolate with everyone.

12 o'clock is also called midday.

Cake and presents

It is time for our party picnic. There are sandwiches, fruit, lemonade and, of course, my birthday cake!

Time for my cake

1 o'clock
Grandma carefully lights the candles on my cake.

Everyone sings 'Happy Birthday' as I blow out the candles. Then we all have a slice of the yummy cake.

More presents!

My friends give me even more presents,
like this amazing watch. I am so lucky,
and say 'thank you'. Now I can
tell the time with my own watch!

Another party game

2 o'clock

My watch says it is 2 o'clock. We still
have 2 hours before we have to go
home. Let's play rounders!

What is your favourite party game?

Party afternoon

We play rounders for an hour. It is great fun.
Afterwards, we all have a drink to cool down.

Time for a goal!

3 o'clock
My party is nearly over. We play football next.
Football is my favourite game.

4 o'clock

We are all a bit tired now. It is time for my friends to go home. They all had a great time today.

One last game

Mum and I play with my new Frisbee. Dad, Grandma and Grandpa tidy up. We must not leave any mess.

Afternoon is the part of day after midday.

Evening and night

I am too tired to cycle home, so Dad puts my bike on the back of the car.
Then we all go back home.

Dinner time

5 o'clock

Dad makes some tasty pasta. It is my favourite dinner.

Outside, the Sun is getting low in the sky.

A special treat

6 o'clock

As a special birthday treat, we have some yummy ice cream for dessert.

Bed time

7 o'clock

After my bath, I go to bed. I wait for Dad to read me a story, but I am so tired, I fall asleep straight away!

What time do you go to bed?

Time facts

When it is night where you are, it is daytime on the other side of the world.

The Earth is always rotating, or spinning like a top. As the Earth **rotates** towards the Sun, we have daytime. As it rotates away from the Sun, we have night time.

World in light

Look at our planet, Earth. You can only see one side of the planet. This side is lit up by the Sun.

As the Earth rotates, it means that it is not always light in the same place on Earth.

Sun

It is always daytime on the side of the Earth that is lit up by the Sun.

On the bright side it is day.

Earth

On the dark side it is night.

Is it day or night now where you are?

Time to remember

Try these fun puzzles to see what you can remember about the time.

What is the time?
Have a look at these clocks. Can you match the right time with the right clock?

8 o'clock

1 o'clock

3 o'clock

Day or night?

Which of these things would you see during daytime?
Which ones would you see at night?

What time of day is it now?

Glossary

Afternoon Afternoon is the time between noon, or 12 o'clock, and dinner time.

Day A day is 24 hours. It starts and ends at midnight. It has a daytime and a night time. Daytime has four parts: morning, noon, afternoon and evening.

Evening Evening is the time between having your dinner and going to bed. Sometimes this is when the Sun is setting, too.

Hour An hour is 60 minutes. There are 24 hours in every day.

Midnight This is 12 o'clock in the middle of the night. It is when days begin and end.

Minute A minute is 60 seconds. There are 60 minutes in an hour.

Morning Morning is the time between when you wake-up and noon.

Night This is the time when it is dark outside and you are in bed.

Noon Noon is the middle of the day. It is 12 o'clock. Sometimes it is called midday.

O'Clock This is used when telling the time. It tells you that the big minute hand is pointing exactly at the 12. The time is exactly the number the little hand is pointing at, such as 8 o'clock.

Rotates Turns around, like a spinning top.

Do you remember what the times on these clocks are?